Spiritual Inspirations

Volume 3

PALMETTO
PUBLISHING
Charleston, SC
www.PalmettoPublishing.com

Hardcover ISBN: 979-8-8229-4288-2
Paperback ISBN: 979-8-8229-4289-9
eBook ISBN: 979-8-8229-4290-5

Spiritual Inspirations

Volume 3

Carol B Pugh

Hope

With God hope is not lost.

Put your trust in God.

Contents

Part 1—Warning

Leech

Beware: there are leeches out there.

Not everyone who comes into our lives
is sent by God.
We fool ourselves.
Beware: there are leeches out there.

We want love, family, and friends.
But people will use you if you let them.
They will attach themselves to you.
They will suck you dry.
Beware: there are leeches out there.

I have met some leeches
in my lifetime.
It is all about what they want,
what they need.
It will never be about you.
Beware: there are leeches out there.

There are so many good people
who fall for the leeches.
A kind heart gets you
nowhere with a leech.

Beware: there are leeches out there.

A leech is always on the move,
looking for a host.
That is how the devil is.
If not you, he will move on.
Beware: there are leeches out there.

Take this warning:
don't let the devil leech on you.
Beware: there are leeches out there.

TO THE SOUL

Are the eyes the windows
to the soul?
What color are your eyes?
Your eyes show you have no soul.

The eyes always tell.
Evil cannot see.
Your eyes are too dark for me.
Your eyes show you have no soul.

Your eyes have no light.
Your soul is dark.
You carry no joy.
God is not within you.
Your eyes show you have no soul.

Can the eyes change?
Can your soul be saved?
Are you condemned?
Do you want out?
Your eyes show you have no soul.

All souls have a chance to be saved.
God has sent Jesus for you.

Will you let the light in?
Your eyes show you have no soul.

It is amazing that Jesus can save you.
Take his hand and let him save you.
Let the light in.
Your eyes show you have no soul.

By saying yes to Jesus,
your eyes will change.
Your soul will bring forth the light.
Light always shines through.
Will you let Jesus in?

A False Disguise

Most people let you see
what they want you to see.
Do you truly know them?
It is likely that you don't.
Are you a wolf in sheep's clothing?

The wolf is always hungry
and ready to eat.
Will the wolf eat you?
Are you a wolf in sheep's clothing?

The devil will disguise himself
as being meek.
The devil is not innocent.
He wants to get close to you.
You are within arm's reach.

Are you a wolf in sheep's clothing?

You must learn how the devil works.
Tricky is his game.
Whether male or female,
the devil wants you.
Are you a wolf in sheep's clothing?

If it acts evil
and slithers like a snake,
it is a snake.
A wolf can put on sheep's clothing,
but it is still a wolf.
Don't let the disguise fool you.
Are you a wolf in sheep's clothing?

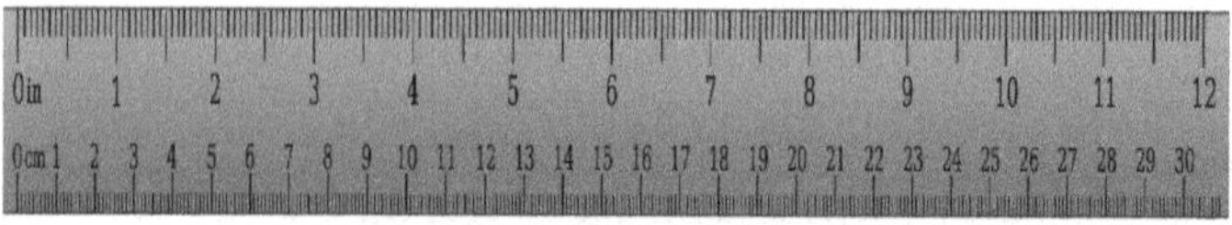

THE MEASUREMENT OF EVIL

Can evil be measured?
How evil can you be?
Evil is winning over me.

Have you passed the devil's test?
Test one: I do not know God.
I pass with flying colors.
The devil is cheering me on.
Evil is winning over me.

Test two: I rebuke Jesus.
My A has just become A+.
The devil is smiling at me.
Evil is winning over me.

Test three: I bow to the devil.
My soul has left me.
I am failing God
but winning with the devil.
Evil is winning over me.

Test four: the devil is my daddy.
I choose the devil. He is my choice.
I follow his lead. Evil has me.
Evil is winning over me.

If you have passed all four tests,
evil has won over you.
Push Replay.
The trick is made for losing.
If you lose against the devil,
you win with God.
Don't let evil win over you.

Player, up. Let's play.

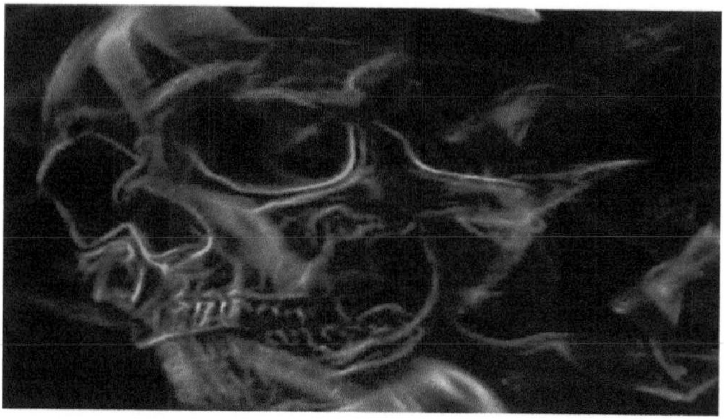

YOU

I saw you in the looking glass.
Could this be you?
Your reflection showed yourself.
I saw you.

No matter how much
you love someone,
that doesn't make them right.
The evil will come through.
Your reflection shows yourself.
I see you.

Evil always wants a cohost.
It wants you to sign the deal.
Evil has no ink.
Your reflection shows yourself.

I see you.

Evil loves to lead. Do not follow.
Your journey will be short.
Evil moves mysteriously.
Your reflection shows yourself.
I see you.

We must stomp out evil
before it spreads.
Evil is like wildfire.
It will consume you.
Do not take evil by the hand.
It will hold you.
Your reflection shows yourself.
I see you.

See evil for what it is.
Run from it if you can.
Your reflection shows yourself.
I see you.

Who the Hero Is

I met a headless hero
who came in a certain form.
He had some wings.
Would I live, or would I die?
This hero was not for me.

He was built like a Titan.
Muscles were everywhere.
He punched with power.
I wanted to be safe.
Would I live, or would I die?
This hero was not for me.

He was the bone crusher,
squashing souls as he goes.
He was the taker of souls.

He was the devil.
Would I live, or would I die?
This hero was not for me.

All heroes are not heroes,
so it seems.
What is the goal of the hero?
Who does the hero defeat?
Would I live, or would I die?
This hero was not for me.

If you see a headless hero,
turn and run;
that hero is not for you.
Have you run?
Will you live, or will you die?

DOOMED

I have eyes of fire.
My soul burns me.
Doomed by life, I was living wrong.

I was so mean
that my look could scare you,
I who had no soul.
I ranked ninety-ninth on the evil scale.
Only the devil ranked higher
than me.
Doomed by life, I was living wrong.

The devil said he wanted
to meet me.
He wanted to shake my hands.
Now that pure evil,
do you know him?
Doomed by life, I was living wrong.

The devil gave me the lifestyle
that I wanted.
The price was my eyes.
I was greedy. I wanted more.
Doomed by life, I was living wrong.

You see, no matter
how much you have,
you will always want more.
Life has hardened me.
Doomed by life, I was living wrong.

I was caught up in worldly things.
I was a keeper of stuff.
I was a collector.
It made no difference to me.
Doomed by life, I was living wrong.

Don't lose yourself to worldly stuff.
It is only material.
Doomed by life, I was living wrong.

HELL WAS CALLING

Do you know evil?
Have you met the dead?
The phone is red.
The number is 666.
A phone that burns.
My ears are burning.

All calls should not be answered.
Let that call go.
Do not leave a voice message.
Unknown caller? Do not accept.
A phone that burns.
My ears are burning.

Your mind will get the best
of you.

You are wondering who is calling.
Like a bill collector,
the number is blocked,
shown only as 666.
A phone that burns.
My ears are burning.

The devil is the seller today.
You are the buyer.
He will be buying
your soul.
The interest rates are up.
Are you for sale?
What is the selling price
of a lost soul?
A phone that burns.
My ears are burning.

Do not call back.
Your fingers will burn.
Do not negotiate;
there is little room for bargaining.
Auction as the winning prize.
A phone that burns.
My ears are burning.

You had to call back.

You resisted the warning.
Sealed by a sale.
Stamped with a number—666.
A phone that burns.
My ears are burning.

THE BOOK OF FLAMES

Have you been living right?
Which book does your name appear?
Red book marked for hell.
Your daddy is calling you.

Time is running out for you.
You chose not to live right.
You were always saying, "Tomorrow."
Tomorrow will not come for you.
Red book marked for hell.
Your daddy is calling you.

You were conceived out of evil.
Your daddy knows you.
You have your daddy's ways:
greed, jealousy, and envy.
Red book marked for hell.
Your daddy is calling you.

How can you think
your name
will be in the good book
marked for heaven?
What good deeds have you done?

None.
Red book marked for hell.
Your daddy is calling you.

Trouble is your middle name.
You are rotten to the core.
Your soul is not clean.
You avert the truth.
Your inside is ugly.
You are a bully.
Out of evil you were born.

Red book marked for hell.
Your daddy is calling you.

Get your name in the good book
of God.
Don't let the devil be your daddy.

GUILTY

You have offended God.
You have broken all his laws.
The price to pay is your life.

You were a repeat offender.
You loved committing sins.
On the first charge you were
let off with a warning.
God said, "Sin no more."
The price to pay is your life.

You went back for more.
You kept sinning.
The second charge was a
misdemeanor.
You were let off light.
God said, "Sin no more."
The price to pay is your life.

You paid no attention
to God's warnings.
You, who discounted God,
continued to sin.
The third charge was a felony.

Three strikes, and you were out.
God said, "Thou have sinned
time and time again."
The price to pay is your life.

Don't let this warning go unnoticed:
the price to pay is your life.

Part 2—Praising

UNREAD STORY

What is the story of your life?
Is it newsworthy?
Will people remember your name?
Unread but a story.

No, I cannot walk on water,
but I can walk tall.
It is story time with Jesus.
Unread but a story.

Some births are so special
that they are on the news,
announcing this child is the one.
Unread but a story.

Some babies are born at home.

Some babies are delivered in the hospital.
This baby was born in a manger.
This child was given to us.
Unto us he was born.
Unread but a story.

From a baby to a boy,
this child lived.
Special. Gifted.
Different from all of us.
Unread but a story.

From a boy to a man,
this child would be.
Name known all over.
Defeated by life, gifted by death.
Unread but a story.

The name that falls on our lips—Jesus.
The story will be told.
Have you read the story of Jesus?

JESUS HEARD

It seems like I am praying
all the time.
When I step forward, you pull me back.
Jesus, can you hear me?

You are stressing me out.
You want to destroy me.
You put your worries on me.
Jesus, can you hear me?

I am glad that I know Jesus.
I start speaking in tongues.
What is this language?
Jesus, can you hear me?

I have a secret.
The password is Jesus.
He is my partner.
Wherever I go, he goes.
Jesus, can you hear me?

It doesn't take much
to activate the password.
When I say his name,

Jesus stands over me.
Jesus, can you hear me?

I knew my voice had been heard
when Jesus told me,
"Stop crying. All is well."
My tears of sadness changed
to tears of joy.
The password had been activated.
Jesus was listening.
Heard by Jesus, saved by Jesus.
Jesus, can you hear me?

Have you been heard by Jesus?
Is your password active?
Jesus, can you hear me?

TRYING

Have you tried Jesus?
Will the world continue spinning without you?
Jesus, I'm still trying.

Do you say his name
when you rise?
If you think, you
rise by yourself,
you still need work.
Jesus, I'm still trying.

With this man life begins.
So I say, "Lord, you are."
You may fall short
but not with Jesus.
Jesus, I'm still trying.

Harm comes
when you don't try.
You will make an excuse
for the reason why.
Trying. I did not try.
Know where the blame lies.
Jesus, I'm still trying.

I choose not to give up.
With Jesus I always can
and always will
It goes without saying
I will never stop trying.
Jesus, I'm still trying.

I keep trying to make it in.
Heaven is the destination.
Jesus and our God will be there.
Jesus, I'm still trying.

Are you trying to make it in?
An attempt is all you need.
Jesus, we are still trying.

MESMERIZING

Have you ever seen the eyes
of Jesus?
His eyes are mesmerizing.
A look that beholds.

The eyes that hold you captive.
The eyes that can see
right through you.
His eyes say it all.
A look that beholds.

When he looks at you,
you know he is looking at you.
I cannot look away.
What is it
that I see in those eyes?

A look that beholds.

When Jesus looks at you,
it is not just a glance,
which you can miss.
I was captivated by his eyes.
His eyes were pulling me in.
I was mesmerized. I kept looking.
A look that beholds.

It is a blessing
when Jesus looks at you.
I did not want Jesus to look away.
Keep looking at me, Jesus.
A look that beholds.

If I am in Jesus's vision,
can I be saved?
He who looks at me
cares for me.
A look that beholds.

Let the eyes
of Jesus mesmerize you.
Are you looking?
A look that beholds.

Selling Jesus

Is Jesus for sale?
Can Jesus be sold?
Is Jesus free
for all to see?
Unsold, cannot be bought.

When it comes to Jesus,
can you put a price on him?
Last time I checked,
Jesus is priceless.
Unsold, cannot be bought.

You may say
a church cannot be run
for free.
A book cannot be given
for free.
Is that selling Jesus?
Unsold, cannot be bought.

It is the story of Jesus
that may be sold.
I am a buyer of Jesus.
I believe in the myth.

I know Jesus has existed.
He still lives.
Unsold, cannot be bought.

Which version have you bought?

JESUS, THE LIGHT

Everyone has their own take
on what Jesus looked like.
If you are white,
Jesus has got to be white.
You can't see yourself
bowing down to one of color.
Can you picture this?

If you are black,
Jesus is black.
Hair like wool, short, and curly.
Flesh of bronze. Eyes on fire.
Built of might.
Can you picture this?

The Bible seldom speaks
of what Jesus looked like.
It is not the features of Jesus
but his message and reasoning
that is important.
Don't lose sight of that.
Can you picture this?

When I saw Jesus,

he wasn't of color.
The form was of a man
emanating light.
Can you picture this?

I feared if I stared too long,
I would be blinded by the light.
I had to look away.
I wanted to see Jesus again.
I was seeing Jesus in his true form.
Can you picture this?

Now for the man Jesus,
consider where he was born.
He could fit into a crowd
and not be recognized.
That speaks volumes.
What color was the family
he was born into?
Can you picture this?

How about this?
Jesus was a poor man born of color
because that what was he needed to be.
Remove the emphasis on the color
and see Jesus as the light.
Can you picture this?

GOD, THE ANCHOR

Have you ever been lost
without hope?
Let God be your anchor.

God is hope.
God guides me. He grounds me.
He is when I am not.
Let God be your anchor.

It takes weight
to hold me down.
That is what God is.
I cannot start my day
without God.
Oh, Lord, I thank thee.
Let God be your anchor.

Life can put you in a hurry.
I am rushing for this,
rushing for that.
Why are we hurrying?
God holds the clock.
Let God be your anchor.

A clock can tick without me.
But my God can stop time.
Isn't that something?
Let God be your anchor.

God made you. Let him hold you.
Stop; stand still.
Take the time to admire God.
Let God be your anchor.

Will you let God anchor you?

DOORS

Is your mindset right?
Are you getting too comfortable
where you are in life,
choosing not to move forward?
Ask yourself, "Am I right?"
God can open doors.
Let him make a way.

Sometimes God must make us move.
God will close a door
to open another.
God can open doors.
Let him make a way.

When you try to do it your way,
nothing happens.
There is a pushback
in getting back.
Get God on your side.
Watch him work.
God can open doors.
Let him make a way.

We tap on doors

when God knocks them down.
When we don't know why,
God knows how.
God can open doors.
Let him make a way.

I need God
to open doors for me.
People will say no
to a simple knock.
It can't be done.
No, we don't need any help
when the Now Hiring sign is out.
God can open doors.
Let him make a way.

I learned my way is not the way.
It is always God's way.
What does God want?
God can open doors.
Let him make the way.

THE REACH

Is the power of God majestic?
The ruler of all rulers.
I would say yes.
The reach of God.
How far is his reach?

Do you think you can hide
from God?
You can do evil,
and he does not see.
God sees all things.
The reach of God.
How far is his reach?

In this world we throw stones.

We turn our heads
and hide our hands,
thinking that God doesn't see us,
making a fool of ourselves.
The reach of God.
How far is his reach?

There is no place you can hide
from God.
A God who can open heaven,
can reach you.
You are a child
trying to rule the Father.
Don't do that.
God carries a wrath.
He is not to be played with.
The reach of God.
How far is his reach?

This God I serve is my God.
The reach of his power
carries no limits.
He is the God
who can snap his fingers,
and the world will cease
to exist.
The reach of God.

How far is his reach?

He is the God whom I turn to
when I am in need.
He makes my life better.
He can reach me
no matter where I am.
The reach of God.
How far is his reach?

When I get scared, I run to him.
Without a full finger, he shields me.
Look at God.
The reach of God.
How far is his reach?

HEAVEN BREAK

Heaven looks so amazing,
an admired sight
that everyone wants to see.
The revelation of God, I want to see it.

Will he be as you imagine him to be?
Will he be old, or will he be young?
The revelation of God, I want to see it.

I know he will be astonishing.
His appearance will reveal
that he is God.
Unseen but known.
The revelation of God, I want to see it.

Everyone is always talking
about Jesus.
But Jesus is always talking
about God.
By my father you are.
The revelation of God, I want to see it.

Will my eyes be able to see him?
Can I look at his face?

The revelation of God, I want to see it.

I want to see the fullness of God.
I long to gaze at him intently.
When I look at God, I will take him in,
a sight that no one has seen.
The revelation of God, I want to see it.

My Father, when I see you,
beautiful will be the word I utter.
The revelation of God, I want to see it.

Part 3—Uplifting

GOD'S LITTLE HELPER

Can someone be too young
to seek God?
How old do you need to be
to know God or long for him?
Will five or six be too young?
I have a youngling
with a yearning for God.

My six-year-old grandbaby
told me she loved God.
Should I doubt her?
Was she following my lead?
I have a youngling
with a yearning for God.

I know God loves children.

I chose to embrace my granddaughter.
I would teach her
how to find her wings.
I have a youngling
with a yearning for God.

She was always bringing God up
to me.
I was happy that one so young
was taking the right direction
toward God.
I have a youngling
with a yearning for God.

I pointed to heaven.
I told her, "God lives there."
She drew a picture
of what she saw,
what heaven looked like
to her.
She told me she wanted
to go there.
I have a youngling
with a yearning for God.

I told her to make room
in her heart for Jesus.

He would guide her
to her heavenly home.
I told her
I would see her there.
Our paths were connected.
I have a youngling
with a yearning for God.

If a child asks you about God,
impart the wisdom
they will need to get to heaven.
You have a youngling
with a yearning for God.

I WANT THE BREAD

Jesus's body was virtual.
His body was the bread.
I want the bread.

Jesus told us *to eat*
of his body.
I want the bread.

Eating of his body
is my bond with Jesus.
His body, the flesh,
was laid down for me.
I want the bread.

His body fills me.
His body made me.
Just a little piece
of his body saved me.
I want the bread.

You should eat of his body
if you want everlasting life.
I will eat the bread.
I want the bread.

THE BLOOD

How powerful is the blood of Jesus?
At the Last Supper,
Jesus told us *to drink his blood.*
I want the blood.

Jesus's blood is protection.
When it runs through your veins,
it feels like fire.
You are alive. You are living.
I want the blood.

I always say, "Cover me
in your blood.
I need the blood of Jesus."
I know what his blood
can do.

It shields me.
I want the blood.

I am empowered
because I am protected
by the blood.
The blood is the juice.
It flows through my body.
I took a sip of Jesus's blood.
I wanted the blood.

Just a sip of the blood
brings forth might.
No bullet can pierce its shield.
I wanted the blood.

I drank Jesus's blood.
I still live.

If you need a shield,
drink the blood of Jesus.
No harm shall come to thee.

Cosigned

How good is your credit?
Good credit, wrong attitude.
You do nothing for no one.
Will Jesus sign for you?

You mistreat people
without a thought.
This world is not yours
to take.
Will Jesus sign for you?

It takes a right being
to do the right thing.
Jesus won't abandon you
in your hour of need.
Will Jesus sign for you?

Are you that special person?
A heart within a heart?
Do your eyes bleed red?
Will Jesus sign for you?

He who looks down on no one
stood for me.

Jesus raised his hands for me.
Will Jesus sign for you?

On Judgment Day God asked,
"Who stands for her?"
Jesus rose to his feet.
He responded with these words:
"My father, I stand for her."
Jesus cosigned for me.

I who thought
I was alone had someone.
I had Jesus on my side.
Jesus cosigned for me.

A GIFT BOX

At times I become so sad.
I feel unwanted and unloved.
I got a gift that came in a box.

There was a knock at my door.
When I opened it,
I only saw a box,
thinking the package had been
misdelivered.
I got a gift that came in a box.

I looked at the box.
It had my name on it.
It was for me.
"Where did it come from?" I thought.
I got a gift that came in a box.

I was thinking, "What is in this box?"
I smiled and said,
"Someone thought about me."
I opened it.
I got a gift that came in a box.

In the box was a rock

that said, "Jesus loves."
My face lit up. I was grinning.
I got a gift that came in a box.

I knew the gift was a message
from Jesus, saying he loves me,
a gift that came in a box.
one that came on time
from above.
I got a gift that came in a box.

If you receive a box, look inside.
It could be a rock sent from above.
I got a gift that came in a box.

WINGED

I got a call from heaven.
My wings were ready.
You would think
I would be happy to get the wings.
But I wanted to know the color.
Do wings come in color?

The angel asked why.
I replied, "I was a visual person.
I loved color; therefore, I
wanted my wings to be colorful."
Do wings come in color?

The angel told me,
"All things are possible in heaven."
I knew then

that my wings would be colorful.
Do wings come in color?

If you get a call from heaven
to get your wings,
ask them,
"What color is yours?"

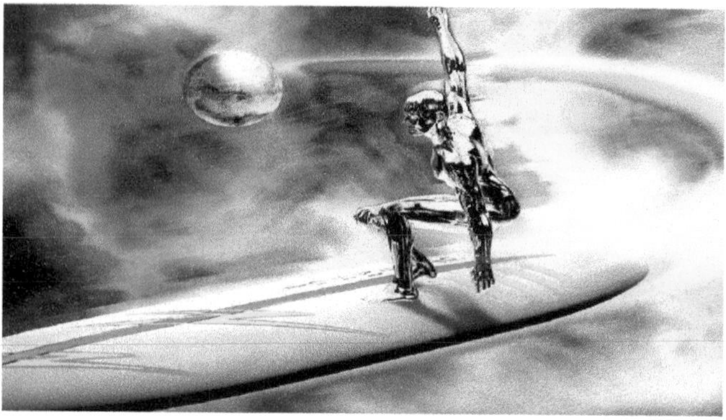

SOUL SURFING

Have you found yourself?
Are you the same?
Have you changed?
I have found my soul. I like who I am.

Sometimes people don't know
who they are.
But they are willing to change.
I have found my soul. I like who I am.

I learn to accept the bad
with the good.
If an apple has a worm,
all is not lost.
When I remove the bad,
only the good is left.

I have found my soul. I like who I am.

Trouble comes in waves.
If it is not one thing, it is another.
If you have no troubles,
you cannot become what you are meant to be.
I have found my soul. I like who I am.

I became
who I wanted to be.
I had to make a change.
If I kept the old me,
there would be no change.
I would be lost.
I was riding the waves.
I have found my soul. I like who I am.

The next time you see a wave,
ride it.
It may take you someplace new
to a better you.
I have found my soul. I like who I am.

ONLY THE CHOSEN

Did you know most people
think they are going to heaven?
Some pastors even try to change
the number of the heavenly bound.
Are you part of the chosen ones?

Believe me,
I want to be included in that number.
It is only for a select few.
What a gift it will be
to be chosen by God.
Are you part of the chosen ones?

Some try to compare their works.
It is not the work.
It is the choice of God that counts.
God sees something in you
that you cannot see in yourself.
God makes you worthy.
Are you part of the chosen ones?

Know this:
you've got to put in the work.
Some will even call you crazy.

People will be jealous of you.
You have God's favor.
Are you part of the chosen ones?

In the past
I wanted to speak
with a chosen one.
I want to know
what it feels like
to speak with God.
I have come to know
the feeling.
I am one of the chosen ones.

I have been chosen by God.
Isn't God good?

If you are chosen by God,
your path will not be easy,
but God will be with you.
Are you part of the chosen one?

CONTAINED BEAST

Are you an animal lover?
It is OK if you are not.
If you were an animal,
what would you be?
I contain the beast within.

My beast is a tiger
that lies dormant within me.
I have mastered my beast.
I rule it.
The beast does not rule me.
I contain the beast within.

I wear a tattoo of my beast
on my leg.
I keep it covered
so others may not see.

I contain the beast within.

Some people act like animals.
They want to be mean.
Their spirits are dark.
They go after others.
If I am provoked,
I sharpen my claws.
I am in attack mode,
but I will not strike.
I contain the beast within.

I get mad, but I calm down.
My beast must sleep.
Please do not awake
the beast within.
It can be dangerous for you.
I contain the beast within.

Try not to let others push you
out of your character.
Your beast may wake up.
Contain the beast within.
Ten, nine, eight, seven, six,
five, four, three, two, one,
your beast is asleep again.
I contain the beast within.

SAVED BY CHRIST

It happened before Christ.
It happened during Christ.
It happened after Christ.
We the people were sinning.
Christ, please save me.

You would think
that during
and after the time of Christ,
people
would have gotten better.
Oh, the devil is a liar.
People love to sin.
They don't want to stop.
Christ, please save me.

Speak the name of Jesus Christ,
and you might get stoned.
People don't want
to hear about him.
If you speak of Christ,
you violate their souls.
Christ, please save me.

We have the wicked
and the pretenders,
those who feign salvation.
Look to the left;
they are the most prominent saved people
you know.
Turn your head slightly
to the right.
See them
for who they really are.

They are liars and cheaters.
Christ, please save me.

I wanted to be saved.
I was willing to be saved.
With Christ the saved me
came forward.
Saved by Christ.

If you want to be saved,
submit to Christ.
You, too,
can be saved by Christ.

Part 4—Motivating

NO VALUE

People place no value
on you
when you mean nothing to them.
I am God worthy. My value is gold.

People will use you if you let them.
Remember, you are nothing to them.
It is all about what you
can do for them.
Sad, right?
I am God worthy. My value is gold.

I realize no one is for me.
I must look after myself. I am alone.
I am God worthy. My value is gold.

I fall back on who I am.
I suck up only to God.
No one else cares for me.
I am God worthy. My value is gold.

In this journey I travel alone.
I have no soulmate.
I default on what I know.

I know God will see me through.
I am God worthy. My value is gold.

Life holds back no punches.
All people are not kind.
I am bigger than life.
I know Jesus.
I am built to last.
My life is eternity.
I am God worthy. My value is gold.

To know Jesus is to know God.
I know him.
I am God worthy. My value is gold.

SLEEPLESS

Not everybody sleeps well at night.
What is on their minds?
Why can't I sleep?
Sleep evaded me.
Jesus kept watch over me.

I could not sleep
because the demons were coming
for me. Or so I thought.
My soul was not lost to me.
I still had feelings.
Sleep evaded me.
Jesus kept watch over me.

I was too scared to sleep,
afraid to close my eyes.
I have been up for days.
My body was losing the fight.
I was shutting down.
Sleep evaded me.
Jesus kept watch over me.

The smart me did not know
Jesus was fighting beside me.

We were fighting off evil
to save a soul.
It was not mine
but yours.
The choice to do battle
comes easy when it's for loved ones.
That is how much Jesus loves you.
He will go into battle for you.
Sleep evaded me.
Jesus kept watch over me.

We who think we are alone
are never on our own.
Jesus battles beside us.
I will also stand and fight for you.
I will die for you.
Lose not your sleep.
Jesus kept watch over me.
He is watching and battling.

The Bowing of Jesus

Jesus loved and respected
his Father.
In his presence Jesus bowed.

God told Jesus to lift his head
so he may see—
see the world for was it was
and for what it could be.
In his presence Jesus bowed.

It was the respect that got me,
a son respecting his father,
not Jesus the child
but Jesus the man who bowed
unto God the Father.
In his presence Jesus bowed.

I've been a child myself.
I was raised to respect.
In these days
children know nothing of it.
If they don't respect you,
how can they respect God?
In his presence Jesus bowed.

Parents, don't neglect your duty to
teach your children about respect.
All graves will not give up their dead.
I am back to teaching.
In his presence Jesus bowed.

GAME TIME

Let's get this started.
I am past due for a win.
I was playing it safe,
losing out on my feat.
Player, up.
Jesus will make me win.

I am a big dog on a little porch.
I need room to run.
If you can hang with Jesus.
let's play.
Game on.
Player, up.
Jesus will make me win.

I'm not scared to place a bet.
Sometimes I win.
Sometimes I lose.
But I am willing
to bet on Jesus.
Player, up.
Jesus will make me win.

I have stars in my eyes.

I need this win.
I am ready to move to the top.
Triumph is at hand.
I will claim this victory.
Player, up.
Jesus will make me win.

Don't just stand back and watch;
get into the game.
If your game time
is now, will you play to win?
Player, up.
Jesus will make me win.

The Scrolls

As a disobedient child,
trouble followed me.
God spoke one word to me.
Stillness.
My life was within the scrolls.

We did not create life.
Life was already here.
Stillness.
My life was within the scrolls.

I was feeling myself.
I wanted to talk back.
My tongue was wagging.
Stillness.
My life was within the scrolls.

God said, "Be still, my child."
Standing still would not hurt me.
I needed guidance in my life.
Who could lead me better
than God himself?
Stillness.
My life was within the scrolls.

You cannot learn
if you do not listen.
I got in line with God.

I knew my Father wanted
what was best for me.
Stillness.
My life was within the scrolls.

Don't just be a name on a scroll.
Let your good deeds
speak for you.
Will God remember you?
Stillness.
My life was within the scrolls.

GOLDEN EYES

I've got gold in my eyes.
My sights are set.
Golden eyes. I see gold.

Some can be fooled by gold dust.
Is it real?
I like fourteen karats.
I like the real stuff.
I may go platinum.
Golden eyes. I see gold.

If Jesus is on the up,
my coming up is a must.
I lie down for no man
because Jesus already laid
his life down for me.
Golden eyes. I see gold.

Because Jesus rose for me,
I rise for him.
Nothing in this life
can keep me down.
Is that gold that I see?
Golden eyes. I see gold.

I believe in who Jesus is.
That means
I am already blessed.

My DNA is real. I've passed the test.
I will take what life has
to offer.
I have nerves of steel.
I don't back down.
My ambitions drive me.
I was made to win.
Golden eyes. I see gold.

With gold in my eyes,
they shine bright.
Golden eyes. I see gold.

Let God shine a path for you.
See gold.

A RACE

How fast can you run?
In which direction?
I race for life.
Which direction is up?

I am a slow starter.
I keep the pace.
If I run too fast,
I will not stay the course.
I will give up.
I race for life.
Which direction is up?

I must time myself.
I am not the first.
But I am not the last.
It's all in the timing.
My pace is my will.
I race for life.
Which direction is up?

I stay within the lane.
If I get sidetracked,
I will lose the race.

I race for life.
Which direction is up?

My race started at birth.
My journey is long.
Slow and steady I run.
I race for life.
Which direction is up?

To the end I run.
Surely I will get there.
What will be my trophy?
Eternal life is my prize.
I race for life.
Which direction is up.

Keep running. The direction is up.
Life is for the living.
The dead cannot live.
I run.

THINKING BIG

This mind of mine knows no peace.
Do your mind and body match?
You can be all pretty on the outside
but jacked up on the inside.
I know a lot of people like that.
I've got to think big.
I've got Jesus on my mind.

Is beauty only in the eye
of the beholder?
I know what beauty looks like.
I love pretty things.
I've got to think big.
I've got Jesus on my mind.

You are only as small
as you think you are.
If you put yourself in a box,
you might not get out.
Who is going to set you free?
I've got to think big.
I've got Jesus on my mind.

I did not want to stay

at the bottom.
It was not for me.
My grave could not hold me.
I've got to think big.
I've got Jesus on my mind.

I heard my calling.
I would be free—
free to live with Jesus.
I was thinking big.
I had to think big.
I had Jesus on my mind.

You, too,
can think big
if you let your mind be free.
I've got to think big.
I've got Jesus on my mind.

My mind is free. I think big.
Big.

AN ELEVATION

Does one need an elevator to go up?
Where is up?
Is it the start of life
or where you end up?
I, who ascended into the heavens,
know up.

Time will always be a part of life.
God is an on-time God.
He was timing me.
God was the teacher.
I was his student.
I, who ascended into the heavens,
know up.

Some days God would be serious
with me.
Some days I thought God was
mocking me.
At times my feelings got hurt.
God needed to show me
who I was.
I, who ascended into the heavens,
know up.

This is how I was elevated.
God established me.
He erased my sins.
God levitated me.
He moved within my circle.
I vowed to be true to him.
God lifted me.
You know that is up.
God was my tailor.
He made me.
God was my investor.
He believed in me.

I obeyed God. I was his pupil.
I was next in time. I went up.
I, who ascended into the heavens,
know up.

If you want to be elevated, be one
with God.
You will go up.

A BOOK

Who are you? What are you about?
Can you write? Can you read?
The understanding of God.
The understanding of self.
The recording of my record.
My name was in the book.

There are so many people
trying to get into heaven.
It all comes down
to a book with names.
The recording of my record.
My name was in the book.

I want my name
to be in that book.

I had to start early
to reach that goal.
The recording of my record.
My name was in the book.

I was taught
heaven wasn't made.
Heaven is.
Do you want to go to heaven?
The recording of my record.
My name was in the book.

To get to heaven,
set your goals high.
Reach for the sky.
Heaven is possible.
The recording of my record.
My name was in the book.

Can I push myself
past my limits?
Yes, I can.
My goal was heaven.
There is no glory without pain.
The recording of my record.
My name was in the book.

I studied the Bible.
I learned about Jesus.
I surrender to Jehovah.
The recording of my record.
My name was in the book.

I observed people.
I learned their ways.
God taught me.
I learned how to care.
Hard work was put in.
Jesus was leading the way.
The recording of my record.
My name was in the book.

Getting to heaven does not come easy.
Will your name be in the book?
Remember, we are all God's people.

Part 5—Inspiring

MADE UP

I saw a dragon.
It looked real to me.
It spoke to me.
Are you looking for the Keeper?

The dragon said, "I am large.
I am fiery. I, too, need a keeper."
As powerful as the dragon was,
he needed help.
Our worlds had collided.
Are you looking for the Keeper?

I asked the dragon, "Are you real?"
The dragon chuckled
at me and said,
"The voice you hear is mine."

Are you looking for the Keeper?

I said, "This must be a fantasy."
It was hard for me
to believe
what I was seeing.
I, too, must be a fantasy.
Am I real?
Are you looking for the Keeper?

I was doubting life.
The dragon said, "Our journey is
the same.
I, the dragon, need a master."
Are you looking for the Keeper?

I asked the dragon, "When I lie
within your wings,
will you comfort me?"
The dragon said,
"That is how it works.
The Keeper puts the strong
with the weak.
God made all."
Are you looking for the Keeper?

I smiled and nested

within the dragon wings.
I told the dragon, "I, too, need help."
I was glad God put me
in the dragon's company
so that differences could become similarities.
I needed the dragon.
The dragon needed me.
We needed each other;
in God we were the same.
Are you looking for the Keeper?

Ask yourself, "Is this real,
or is this made up?"
Let not your differences
separate you.
Are you looking for the Keeper?

DENTED

No one is perfect.
If you walk around as if you are
above everyone else,
your armor carries a dent.

When you are high and mighty
and think you don't need no one else,
that's when God steps up.
God's going to examine you.
Your armor carries a dent.

How can you come
from Adam and Eve
and have no dents?
You are dented.
I can see your flaws.

I, too, wanted to be perfect.
Your armor carries a dent.

I know people are people.
There are the haves
and the have-nots.
Are you one of the
have-nots?
The ones who have
no love and compassion?
Your armor carries a dent.

When your armor cracks,
will you break?
Will I care when you fall?
Your armor carries a dent.

I am the type of person you
want in your corner, a *godsend*.
I will show up
when you need me.
I will be there.
Your armor carries a dent.

When you cry, I am your tear.
God has sent me.
I will be your strength

when you have no other.
Your armor carries a dent.

I am your friend, your
sister and brother.
If it comes down to it, I will be
your mother.
I am whatever you need me
to be.
Your armor carries a dent.

Remember this
when others come to slay you:
no one is perfect.
Be your best self;
that is all you can be
because your armor carries a dent.

Fading

At times do you wish
you could disappear?
Unseen and unheard.
No one listens to you.
I get this feeling
that I can disappear.
I am fading away.

You have lost your will.
You live under another.
You have lost your individuality.
I get this feeling
that I can disappear.
I am fading away.

You know not the beginning
nor the ending.
Where did I go wrong?
I get this feeling
that I can disappear.
I am fading away.

I have been torn down,
ripped into pieces.

Someone is mistreating me.
Is it life, or is it just me?
I get this feeling
that I can disappear.
I am fading away.

Just when I thought,
there was no life left in me,
I encountered Jesus.
He kissed me on the forehead
and said, "This life is yours."

My life was given to me
by God.
This is my life to live.
I stop fading. I start living.

Please don't let anyone
make you fade away.
God wants you to live.

MASKED

Who is behind the mask?
Do I smile, or do I cry?
Unmasked. I hid behind the mask.

Do you even know yourself?
I know not myself.
I am always in disguise,
unknown even to myself.
Unmasked. I hid behind the mask.

I was born a Gemini;
therefore, two live within me.
One part of me smiles,
while the other cries.
Torn from within.
Unmasked. I hid behind the mask.

Can I find oneness within myself?
Jesus said I could.
Jesus told me, "Wrestle no more
within yourself. I will set you free."
Unmasked. I hid behind the mask.

With those words

I made peace within myself.
My mind and body could rest.
I was unmasked.
Seen by Jesus, I was set free.
Unmasked. I hid behind the mask.

Live without a mask.
Let Jesus set you free.
Unmasked. I hid behind the mask.

Rising Phoenix

I enjoyed God's favor.
It only took God one day
to rebirth me.
I turned sixty, still a baby
to God.
I, the phoenix, had risen.

The devil sent you to me,
you who plotted against me.
It was easy for you to team up
with the devil.
Jealousy and envy held you.
I, the phoenix, had risen.

I did not think
that you would choose

to hurt me.
Your heart was black.
Where did you come from?
Who made you?
Return from
whence you came.
Out of darkness I rose.
I, the phoenix, had risen.

You who stood beneath me,
you wanted to be me.
You spit hatred on me.
You, of all people,
wanted to harm me.
I, the phoenix, had risen.

I wanted to thank you
for helping God rebirth me.
Without you
I would not have been reborn.
I, the phoenix, had risen.

After twenty-four hours, I was made new.
I had to cry. I cried for myself.
My Father heard me.
He increased my strength
tenfold as a gift.

Watch out, I am strong.
I, the phoenix, has risen.

Out of the flames I rose.
My voice changed.
My words transformed.
I, who carried God's might,
stood.
I, the phoenix, had risen.

ACCOUNTABILITY

When trouble comes,
do you point your finger
at someone else?
I hold myself accountable .
I bear the burden of my own guilt.

I learned the difference
between right and wrong
when I was a child.
I know the difference
between Jesus and God.
One is the Father.
The other is the Son.
I hold myself accountable.
I bear the burden of my own guilt.

To get to where I am going,
I took responsibility for my own actions.
I must live my life according
to God's laws.
I hold myself accountable.
I bear the burden of my own guilt.

My husband and children

cannot get me into heaven.
It will take Jesus
and my own doing.
I must think past me
and think about him.
I hold myself accountable.
I bear the burden of my own guilt.

I must look at the big picture,
and not the small details.
The corner is only a piece
of the big picture.
I am thinking big.
I am thinking of the past,
the present, and the future.
I hold myself accountable.
I bear the burden of my own guilt.

If I want to make it to heaven,
I must get past me and you.
I am going to do right
by me and by God.
I hold myself accountable.
I bear the burden of my own guilt.

To make it to heaven,
you must do the right thing.
Hold yourself accountable.

The Making of an Angel

What does it take to be an angel?
Are angels born, or are they made?
Born human, made an angel.

So many stories have been told.
Does your spirit flee from thee?
Born human, made an angel.

It takes great work to be an angel.
It demands your spirit and enthusiasm.
Your heart must evolve.
Born human, made an angel.

If I told you the truth,

would you believe me?
The truth could pass you by.
Ye of little faith
know not who speaks to thee.
Born human, made an angel.

My wings are itching
to get out of my body.
I behold my wings.
Born human, made an angel.

Is your body itching?
Do your wings want out?
Born human, made an angel.

A Face

People in a group
will not see the same thing.
Is it the mind or the eyes
that see?

I see a face within the clouds.
Whose face do I behold?
Can you see?
Is it the mind or the eyes
that see?

I see the world held
within the light.
What is it that you perceive?
Is it the mind or the eyes
that see?

I see a woman within the sky.
Whose mother is she?
She looks down
from above at me.
Is it the mind or the eyes
that see?

Does my mind tell me
what I see?
Whose arms reach out for me?
Is it the mind or the eyes
that see?

If you are confused
by what you see,
step back and take another look
at the scene.
Is it God or an angel
that you see?

My mind and eyes
play games with me.
Is it the mind or the eyes
that see?

Are you amazed by what you see?
Look around. Can you see
the greatness of God in you and me?
Is it the mind or the eyes
that see?

BRIGHT LIGHT

What is in your heart?
Does your heart pump blood or oil?
You should always know
what is within you.
The shining of a light.

Are you so mean spirited
that your light won't shine?
If you are, I've got a flashlight
for you.
The devil prospers
in the darkness.
The shining of a light.

I want to check how bright
your light shines.

First does your heart pump,
or is it just beating?
If it only beats,
you have no light.
The shining of a light.

Second what is the size
of your heart?
Is it a small heart
that preaches hatred?
Are the words that come
out of your mouth
spoken in poor taste?
If so, you still don't have
a light,
not even a glimpse.
The shining of a light.

Third you have a small heart,
but you are always generous.
You are willing to go without
to help another.
Your light has just become dim.
You have some light.
The shining of a light.

Fourth and in the running

your heart is oversize,
so big that you will miss out
on a lot.
Your big heart just put you
in the running.
Your beam is almost always on.
The shining of a light.

Have you reached the fifth level?
You will know it when you are there.
Jesus is the light.
He always shines through.
You have lost control
of how you shine
because you will always glisten
with Jesus.
The shining of a light.

Bright light, bright light.
Jesus is the light.
Let Jesus shine.

Stepping It Up

Everybody always wants Jesus
to step up for them.
They think Jesus owes them.
The question is,
Can you step up for Jesus?
I'm stepping it up.

I would ask Jesus for
any and everything.
I would be selfish with Jesus.
Never even considered
what Jesus wanted.
I thought Jesus was
a genie in a lamp.
All my wishes would be granted.
I'm stepping it up.

When I stepped it up, I knew
I was not the leader.
I was willing to follow.
I had to become meek.
I put my wants and needs aside.
It was all about Jesus's will.
Whatever Jesus was willing

to give me, I would accept it.
I'm stepping it up.

I had to prove myself to Jesus.
I could not stand beside him.
I was not Jesus's equal.
I could not get in front of him.
Jesus set the pace.
I was in his footsteps.
I could barely follow.
I'm stepping it up.

I thought only of Jesus.
Every second to the minute.
Every minute to the hour.
Every hour to the day.
I was beneath myself.
That did not bother me.
It was a meeting of the spirits.
I knew exactly
what Jesus wanted.
No words had to be spoken.
I was in tune with Jesus.
I'm stepping it up.

Can you put yourself aside
and become like Jesus?

I stepped it up.

I followed Jesus; will you?

PART 6—LOVING

THORNY LOVE

Do you find love,
or does love find you?
Are you looking for a mate
or for a lover?
I had a love that came with thorns.

Sometimes love comes too easy.
I want to know what true love is.
Finding true love takes time.
Your love got me questioning,
what love is.
I had a love that came with thorns.

I don't want to lose
at this thing call love.
My heart is at stake.

I want love
to want me.
Can I find my true love?
My forever love?
I had a love that came with thorns.

Your love was a rose
that came with thorns.
You were the ruler
of your love;
your love wasn't free.
Where there are thorns
there is blood.
You made my heart bleed.
I had a love that came with thorns.

I rushed through love.
Love is not simple.
A thorny rose will prick you.
Beautiful to see, difficult to hold.
I had a love that came with thorns.

I should have prayed
before this love.
Jesus sends me a love
that I can love.
I had a love that came with thorns.

I am counting on Jesus
to send my true love.
I had a love that came with thorns.

MISSING OUT

Is there anything better
than love?
Love is all I have.
To give love, to be loved.
I loved you with all of me.

Love can let you down.
Sometimes love is not enough.
I loved you with all of me.

I loved you with every fiber of my being.
You were my world.
You made it hard for me to love.
I loved you with all of me.

Life does not stop with you,
one man devoid of love.
In the name of love,
will you love?
Can you love?
I loved you with all of me.

You mistakenly think you are
a loser in love, but you are not.

He is the one missing out.
He threatens to leave you.
Let him go.
Jesus has someone better for you.
I loved you with all of me.

You mourn for
the time you spent
Don't cry over spilled milk.
You have loved and lost.
You will love someone again.
I loved you with all of me.

Sometimes you will love many times.
There is the second time around.
My grandmother was married five times.
Oh, she had that loving feeling.
I loved you with all of me.

In the end
put your love in God's hands.
Stop missing out.

A LIMITLESS LOVE

I want a love that
has no condition.
I want a love
just because.
Why do you love me?
Because.
Let me be your only one.

I want to love you
willingly.
I want you to think of me
when you think of love.
I will be your Yum-yum.
Let me be your only one.

Love is not a cell
if it can be free.
It will carry no limit.
I became your past.
I was tamed by love.
I didn't want to be free.
Let me be your only one.

Unreachable, unmoved,
I was taken by love.

Let me be your lullaby.
I pledge my love.
Let me be your only one.

Like Jesus, my love has no limit.
I will love you when the sun rises.
I will love you when the sun sets.
I will love you
to the moon and back.
Let me be your only one.

Played Love

Do you play the fool for love?
The games that people play.
A spicy love that burns like fire.
Your love runs hot to me.
How long does the fire burn?

Is this love or lust?
Does love end eventually?
If so,
will your love lust for me?
How long does the fire burn?

I was an innocent child
when you gave your love to me,
thinking, "Oh what a love
you must have for me."
I was the favorite toy.
You loved to play with me.
How long does the fire burn?

My youth was against me.
I lost my innocence.
Did I grow too old?
How long does the fire burn?

I was candy to you. You love sweets.
We played house with our love.
Were we pretending?
Was there kindling for your fire?
I put wood in the flames.
How long does the fire burn?

We both played the game.
Were we in love?
Bonded by God
our love would not go under.
How long does the fire burn?

Young and in love.
How long does the fire burn?

Heartbeat

If you lay your hands
on my chest,
you can feel my heart beating.
If you listen closely,
you can hear my heartbeat.
Skip, skip!
My heart is missing a beat.

How big is your heart?
Is there room for love?
Can love fill your heart?
Skip, skip!
My heart is missing a beat.

Pain is not good for the heart.
It leaves no room for love.
My heartbeat is my rhythm.
It is music to my ears.
Skip, skip!
My heart is missing a beat.

An overfilled heart
leaves no room for Jesus.
I was out of step with him;

therefore, my heart
was missing a beat.
Can I get my rhythm back?
Skip, skip!
My heart is missing a beat.

Be still, my heart.
I just made room for Jesus.
I got my joy back.
I am back in rhythm with Jesus.
Skip, skip!
My heart didn't miss a beat.

If you find your heart
missing a beat,
try filling it with Jesus.
Skip, skip!
My heart was missing a beat.

PRECIOUS LOVE

How far can love carry you?
I had a precious love
that could not last.
Your love was vain to me.
Vanity, oh this love is lost to me.

You were the stars in the sky
and my heaven.
Your love was precious to me.
But your heart turned cold toward me.
Vanity, oh this love is lost to me.

The expression "I want
to love you for a lifetime"
was nothing to me.
My love was stronger than that.
Vanity, oh this love is lost to me.

I saw the real you.
You would not love me back.
You loved yourself too much
for that.
My love was in vain for you.
Vanity, oh this love is lost to me.

In the end it came down
to me.
I learned to love myself
as Jesus loved me.
Now that is an unspeakable love.
His love is not in vain.

Now look in the mirror.
See yourself as Jesus does.
Know that love loves you.
Don't let your love be in vain.

Love someone as Jesus does.
Be a precious stone.

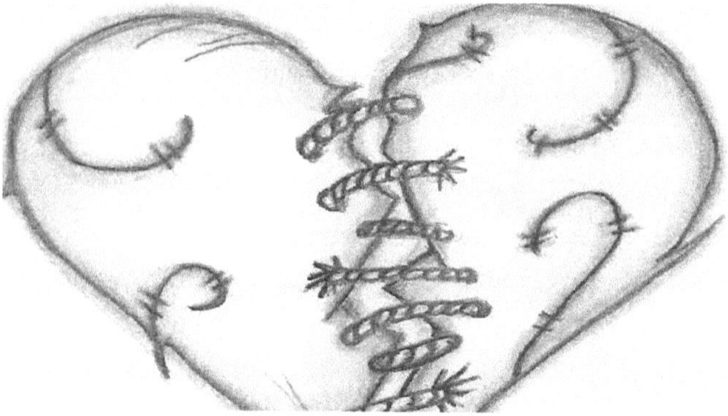

STITCHES

Does love comes and go
like a revolving door?
Is love made up?
Stitches. My love is worth patching.

How often can a heart be broken?
I am running out of thread.
My stitches are overlapping.
Stitches. My love is worth patching.

Are you sad
when you choose not to love?
Someone has mistreated you.
Is there a needle in your eye?
Your heart is at a loss.
Stitches. My love is worth patching.

A scared heart.
What wound do you carry?
You keep hurting. I keep stitching.
Stitches leave marks
for my heart to bear.
Stitches. My love is worth patching.

No ego, no pride.
Is there hope for me?
With Jesus there is always hope.
Love always finds a way.
Let Jesus heal your heart.
He will not leave a mark.
Stitches. My love is worth patching.

Bondage Love

Have you ever had a love
too strong for love?
It consumed you.
What type of love is that?
I was a slave to my own love.

Is love a hundred percent?
Will you settle for 50 percent?
I need love. How about you?
I was a slave to my own love.

You are a predator.
You like to play with your prey.
You like having the upper hand.
You love the challenge of the hunt.
I was the game in your quest.
I was your prey.
I was a slave to my own love.

I know my heart.
I know my desire.
I want satisfaction.
Can you satisfy me?
I was a slave to my own love.

I knew not love with you.
I was your meal. I was your mean.
This love was not true to me.
My heart was missing me.
I was a slave to my own love.

I thought there was something
wrong with me,
choosing me and not you.
A greater love was waiting for me.
I invested my love in Jesus.
I was a slave to my own love.

My love left this world.
My love surpassed boundaries.
Nothing can hold him.
I'm in love with Jesus.
I was a slave to my own love.

You may think of me as a slave.
I wanted Jesus to be my master.
Therefore, I surrendered
all my love to Jesus.
I was a slave to my own love.

If you want a love

that is out of this world,
try loving Jesus.
Be a slave to your own love.

A DATE WITH JESUS

Have you ever been
on a blind date?
I got an invitation
to a masquerade ball.
I didn't know
who my date would be.
I was excited.
I got a date with Jesus.

I was saying to myself, "What
will he look like?
Will he be a gentleman?"
I had so many questions
with no answers.
I was making myself nervous.
I got a date with Jesus.

I would wear my mask
like a crown.
I wanted to impress my date.
I wanted him to remember me.
I was a thing of beauty.
I had to be handled with care.
I got a date with Jesus.

My driver showed up,
but he was in a chariot.
I asked, “What is this?”
I looked closely.
The driver had wings.
I got a date with Jesus.

Being me, I tried to get off.
The driver told me
to have no fear.
Being simple-minded, I did
not know the driver was an angel.
I got a date with Jesus.

The angel took me to heaven
and told me
that Jesus wanted to see me.
An invitation to heaven.

I met him.
I got a date with Jesus.

We laughed. We talked.
Jesus told me
my long-suffering had ended.
I had a taste of heaven.
I got a date with Jesus.

If you want a date
with Jesus, get an invitation
to heaven.
You may see Jesus.

LETTING GO

Would you rather lose at love
or lose a loved one?
When is it OK to let go?
I don't know how
to surrender.
To save myself I must let go.

A loss can devastate you.
It is hard to move on.
You resist
what you must do.
To save myself I must let go.

God gives us time to mourn.
But we can't grieve too long.
Remember, God is a jealous God.
He wants all your attention.
To save myself I must let go.

Memories are good.
It allows you to reflect.
Life is funny like that.
One moment I am sad.
The next moment I am happy.

Am I going mad?
Can I be both happy and sad?
To save myself I must let go.

When you think
you cannot go any farther,
and you can't take it anymore,
let God push you forward.
You have just been blessed.
To save myself I must let go.

I had to take
this blessing of life,
which God had given me.
I refocused my energy.
I was getting better.
I was surrendering.
To save myself I must let go.

When a loss make you
lose yourself,
God will make things better.
You must surrender.
Will you let go?

Part 7—Magnifying

DELIVERANCE

What does *deliverance* mean
to you?
Out of bondage came forth a slave.

People suffer in many ways.
You think, "Why is there suffering
if God is real?"
Held captive against your will.
Out of bondage came forth a slave.

When did change truly arrive?
People quickly think
of Moses, the slave.
Yes, Moses was part of the deliverance.
He carried the torch during his time.
God performed many miracles through Moses.

Out of bondage came forth a slave.

My deliverance had to be through Jesus.
The pain Jesus and I suffered
counted for something.
We passed the test.
It brought me closer to the Deliverer.
Out of bondage came forth a slave.

I know
this is not an ordinary man,
he who can deliver me.
Out of bondage came forth a slave.

This is what *deliverance* means:
D is for *death*,
one that was felt
around the world.
Out of bondage came forth a slave.

E is for *earth*.
The death of Jesus happened on the earth.
Out of bondage came forth a slave.

L is for *lives*.
By his death Jesus saved all our lives.
Out of bondage came forth a slave.

I is for *impression*.
Jesus left an impression
on this world in everything he did.
Out of bondage came forth a slave.

V is for *vulnerable*.
As powerful as Jesus was,
he was vulnerable because he cared.
Out of bondage came forth a slave.

The second *E* is for *easy*.
The way to the kingdom is easy
with Jesus. He is a must.
Out of bondage came forth a slave.

R is for *residence*.
Will my home be heaven or paradise?
Jesus resides in my heart.
Out of bondage came forth a slave.

A is for *acknowledgment*.
You must acknowledge Jesus
as your Savior.
Out of bondage came forth a slave.

N is for *never*.
Death will never come again.
Out of bondage came forth a slave.

C, as you might have guessed, is for *choice*.
Jesus had a choice.
He didn't have to die, but he did.
Jesus chose us.
Out of bondage came forth a slave.

The final *E* is for *everlasting*,
the gift of eternal life.
Will we live forever?
The choice is ours.
Jesus is the Deliverer.
Out of bondage came forth a slave.

They Made Jesus Cry

How hurt did Jesus have to be
to weep?
They made Jesus cry.
The tears were blood.

Even a strong man can sob.
Sometimes when people cry, they
don't do it for themselves.
They cry for you.
Jesus was that kind of man.
They made Jesus cry.
The tears were blood.

Crying for a cause.
Our burdens weigh heavily on him.
They made Jesus cry.

The tears were blood.

A weak man would have given in.
Jesus said, "I must complete this task.
My journey comes to an end."
They made Jesus cry.
The tears were blood.

Jesus laid his hands
on his chest.
His heart was still beating.
His blood was still flowing.

Jesus said, "Let this be.
My death will complete me."
They made Jesus cry.
The tears were blood.

In the death
of Jesus, were our hands clean?
They made Jesus cry.
The tears were of blood.

The Killing of Christ

If you witnessed a murder
or know of one, would
you tell?
Who would you inform?
The killing of Jesus.

In today's laws
there is no statute of limitations
for murder.
They killed Jesus back then,
and they are still killing him
time and time again.
I need to make a statement
on the murder of Jesus.
The killing of Jesus.

I went down to the jailhouse.
I told the law
a crime had been committed.
I saw a murder.
They asked, "Whose?"
I stated, "Jesus."
The killing of Jesus.

They asked, "How did it happen?"
I stated, "By false
witness and prosecutions."
Not only did they lie about Jesus
but they also denied him.
They stood still and watched.
No one stood for Jesus
for fear of guilt by association.
The killing of Jesus.

They beat Jesus. I saw blood.
Jesus was small in stature
but had a big heart.
He had the heart of million
with room for more.
The killing of Jesus.

Yes, Jesus carried his own cross
and didn't fight back.
But that was for you and me.
When death did not
come quick,
they pierced his side.
The killing of Jesus.

They told me
the crime did not happen

in their jurisdiction.
I said, "Oh no."
It had been written in the Bible.
I asked, "Are you denying Jesus?"
The killing of Jesus.

I said, "I know the murderers.
If not them,
then who's going to pay?
Maybe their offspring.
Someone needs to pay."
The killing of Jesus.
A crime was committed.

Resurrected

I believe in the resurrection
of Jesus.
Jesus could not die for nothing.
The purification of Jesus.
Jesus said he was purified.

For if Christ be not risen,
my faith would be in vain.
I would still be in sin.
The purification of Jesus.
Jesus said he was purified.

Jesus was already pure.
He had to return
to who he was.
The purification of a God.

His grave was empty.
The purification of Jesus.
Jesus said he was purified.

Who moved the rock?
It was the voice of God
calling his Son's name.
"Rise, my son."
The purification of Jesus.
Jesus said he was purified.

I carry the belief
that Jesus, the Son, rose.
The purification of Jesus.
Jesus said he was purified.

If you believe Jesus rose to heaven,
look up and nod.
The purification of Jesus.
Jesus said he was purified.

CROWNED

Do you feel royal?
Do you feel privileged?
Are you worthy of a crown?

Are you a queen or a king?
Do you wear the crown?
Are you worthy of a crown?

What does it take
to wear a crown?
Jesus, the King, dons one.
He who wears the crown
is enthroned.
He is worthy of the crown.

Jesus, the Son of God,
wears his crown.
I know no other worthy
of it.
Jesus's crown is heavenly.
No other has ruled so many.
He is worthy of the crown.

Jesus was born to be King.

He who would be crowned
is my King.
He is worthy of the crown.

Even in death
Jesus wore the crown.
It was the sign
that he would be King.
He is worthy of the crown.

King Jesus is crowned.
He is worthy of his crown.

THE MYSTERY OF THE BLOOD

What does it take to save a life?
Is it the heart, or is it the blood?
The man who cried blood.
Who do I serve?

I asked myself,
"What was in the blood?"
The blood was spiritized with purity.
It made the heart pure
through freedom from sin and evil.
The man who cried blood.
Who do I serve?

The blood carries an odor.
It smells of undefeatable strength.
It leaves a trail
that all may follow.
His blood paves the way.
The man who cried blood.
Who do I serve?

I said to Jesus, "If I were a
vampire, I would suck

your blood."
Jesus responded,
"My blood I give to thee."
The man who cried blood.
Who do I serve?

I serve Jesus.
The man who cried blood.
Who do you serve?

MIRACLES

A miracle is something wonderful,
extraordinary, and supernatural.
Jesus was the miracle.

Birth by a virgin mother.
How was that possible?
Who was the father?
Jesus was the miracle.

Most people focus
on the miracles
Jesus performed
when the miracle was Jesus.
Keep your eyes on him.
Jesus was the miracle.

Jesus was never childless.
He was the child,
a miracle child
who was sent.
Jesus was the miracle.

Did you know miracles can grow?
Jesus grew into that man.
He was awesome.
Look at a miracle.
Look at Jesus.
Jesus was the miracle.

Sitting High

I have a bird who loves to sit high.
He watched me from above.
He is sitting high on his cage.
He who sits high commands me.

When he speaks, I listen.
He warns me when harm is near.
He who sits high commands me.

It made me think,
"God watches over me.
He sits high on his throne."
He who sits high commands me.

Simply living life,
at times I am careful.
But all of us can be careless,
making mistakes as we go.
He who sits high commands me.

When God sees trouble, he shields me.
My Father protects me.
Yes, I am my Father's child.
He who sits high commands me.

I must pay attention to my Father.
If I forget to do so,
he taps me.
I, the child, must get in line.
He who sits high commands me.

I smile and ask my Father,
"What should I do today?
I am at your command."
He who sits high commands me.

There is order in my Father's house.
Jehovah, you who sit high command me.
I know my place with my Father.
He who sits high commands me.

THE LETTER *S*

The letter *S* goes with God.
God comes with an *S*.

God wants you to be his subject.
He wants you to submit to him.
God comes with an *S*.

You must submerge yourself in God.
Surrender to him.
You cannot be stubborn with God.
God is not having it.
God comes with an *S*.

God will summon you
with a subpoena.
You must appear before him.
God is strict with what he does.
God comes with an *S*.

If you are God's student,
he will give you
the strength to survive.
He will be your Savior.

God comes with an *S*.

God is your safety net.
He will show up when you call.
His Spirit is in your soul.
God comes with an *S*.

God sacrificed Jesus for us.
Oh, the letter *S* is strong.
God comes with an *S*.

Saints, behold your Father.
God comes with an *S*.

APPRECIATION

When someone helps you,
should you say "thank you"?
He who blessed me, I thank thee.

Appreciation is a word
that means thankfulness.
I recognize you.
You know where
your help comes from.
He who blessed me, I thank thee.

I take no credit
for the help I receive from someone else.
They come
in my time of need.
That's how God is.
He who blessed me, I thank thee.

I want to award
a certificate of appreciation to God.
I want to show him that I am grateful.
He who blessed me, I thank thee.

I proudly present

this certificate
to *Jehovah, the Almighty God*
for your dedication and kindness to me,
a loyalty that cannot be bought.
You have loved and cared for me.
Your blessings are many.
Jehovah, I thank thee.

Part 8—Healing

TRAPPED

I live a lie.
My soul is unhappy with me.
There is no escape for me.

I am alive, but I don't live,
held hostage within myself.
There is no escape for me.

This hold is bonded to me.
I cannot breathe. I gasp for air.
This demon stands on me.
Please get off me.
I want to be free.
There is no escape for me.

Your darkness overshadows me.

I am tired of your threats.
I just want to be free.
There is no escape for me.

I have no one to turn to.
I sit alone. I cry to myself.
Can I be free?
There is no escape for me.

I know freedom is not mine.
I've made bad choices in my life.
I am confined
in a cell with no room to breathe.
There is no escape for me.

I am confined from within.
I have no words.
This demon contains me.
There is no escape for me.

If you are reading this,
please pray for me.
There is no escape for me.
My sadness has overcome me.
There is no escape for me.

Does Jesus hold the key

to this cell?
Can I run and tell?
Trapped by society.
But Jesus unchained me.

I escaped my cell. Let Jesus free you.
He holds the keys.

UNCONTAINABLE

Have you ever felt caged?
Locked up with nowhere to go?
Caged by your mind.
Caged by society.
Caged by a loved one.
With unclipped wings I can fly.

What gets you down?
Are you chained? Are you isolated?
With unclipped wings I can fly.

Only by going through the lows,
can you truly enjoy the highs.
I want to go high.
Can you fly?
With unclipped wings I can fly.

Can you accept what life has
to offer?
I have no roses in my hands.
Life will not break me.
With unclipped wings I can fly.

Who stands on your back?
Who holds your key?
Are you in despair?
With unclipped wings I can fly.

I who chose to stand
is still standing.
I have broken my chains.
I am free to fly.
With unclipped wings I can fly.

Free yourself so you can fly.

CONFINED BUT NOT HELD

How dark is your mind?
Will your mind let you see?
God created something
when he created me.
Confined by a mind.
Freed by intelligence.
My mind runs free with me.

The mind is the master
of the body.
The heart can feel.
But it cannot lead.
Confined by a mind.
Freed by intelligence.
My mind runs free with me.

Does your mind go dark?
Have you been convicted
by your own mind?
Confined by a mind.
Freed by intelligence.
My mind runs free with me.

Do you struggle within yourself?
A battle within a battle.
Will I win?
Confined by a mind.
Freed by intelligence.
My mind runs free with me.

My mind controls all
my emotions.
The greatness within a mind.
My mind sets the tone.
Confined by a mind.
Freed by intelligence.
My mind runs free with me.

Can you be outsmarted
by your own mind?
My mind is working against me.
Confined by a mind.
Freed by intelligence.
My mind runs free with me.

A mind can break under pressure.
How strong is your mind?
Confined by a mind.
Freed by intelligence.
My mind runs free with me.

Does God guide your mind?
I could not control my own psyche.
I humble myself before God.
I put God in control.
God freed my mind.
Confined by a mind.
Freed by God.
My mind runs free with me.

THE TUNE-UP

Do you drive?
Do you own a car?
Will a car breaks down?
Jesus is the owner of this ride.

Can life be your ride?
Like a car I will glide.
Jesus is the owner of this ride.

Can that which is broken be fixed?
Down on luck, down on life.
Will I abandon this car?
My mind, body, and soul.
Jesus is the owner of this ride.

I don't sell myself short.
I know I need a tune-up.
I'm getting an oil change.
I will change things up.
A car that does not work
can be fixed.
Jesus is the owner of this ride.

My spark plugs did not fire.
The alternator had no light.
I was lost and abandoned.
Jesus is the owner of this ride.

My body was the car.
Jesus was the auto mechanic.
Every now and then
I backslid in my faith.
I lacked the tools
to sustain my belief.
Jesus is the owner of this ride.

To stay whole
you must get a tune-up.
Jesus had a fix on my life.
Jesus is the owner of this ride.

A used car can be driven.
It is not new but usable.
The words
of the Bible are my gas.
Will you ride?
Jesus is the owner of this ride.

If your vehicle has broken down,
let Jesus be your auto mechanic.

Life will go on.

Jesus is the owner of this ride.

Popcorn

When cooking popcorn,
some kernels do not pop.
Some even burn.
Jesus was the butter to my popcorn.

You can go through a dry spell
in life.
Nothing is popping.
I wanted something to happen.
I needed some action.
Jesus was the butter to my popcorn.

How do you pop your kernels
on top of the stove
or in the microwave?
All kernels should pop.
When life gets hard,
your kernels will not pop.
Jesus was the butter to my popcorn.

I like butter with my popcorn.
Plain ones are always dry.
They can stick in your throat.
That is not good for you.

A little lube always works.
Jesus was the butter to my popcorn.

In life
we all can use a helping hand.
Jesus is that advocate.
He will make it work.
Jesus was the butter to my popcorn.

LIFELINE

If you saw your life flash
before you, what would you do?
Would you swim, or would you drown?
I needed a lifeline.
Jesus threw me a rope.

I was a small fish in a big pond.
I could not swim. I was madly paddling.
Life was drowning me.
I needed a lifeline.
Jesus threw me a rope.

I did not want to eat worms.
I wanted a steak.
My head was just
above the water. I needed air.
I needed a lifeline.
Jesus threw me a rope.

Where do I go from here?
Beneath the pond is mud.
You can get stuck in it.
Mud is like quicksand.
It can suck you up.

I needed a lifeline.
Jesus threw me a rope.

The rope was made of Jesus's blood.
It surrounded me.
The rope was my life jacket.
I did not go under.
I needed a lifeline.
Jesus threw me a rope.

Some people learn to float
before they swim.
Jesus is my lifeguard.
He always comes to the rescue.
I needed a lifeline.
Jesus threw me a rope.

If you find yourself drowning in life,
let Jesus be your lifeguard.
Saved by a lifeline, you will float.
I needed a lifeline.
Jesus threw me a rope.

Comfortable

How do you react to others?
What spirit do you carry?
Were you born to mistreat,
not caring for another?
I got comfortable. God shook me up.

Do you play with the word *hurt*?
Do you care if you hurt another?
If God is
a loving God, why do you hurt?
I got comfortable. God shook me up.

Do you live just to hurt?
A purpose to do harm.
Your aim is wrong.
Are you a part of God's plan?
I devised a strategy
to do God's will.
I plan to do the right thing.
I got comfortable. God shook me up.

Holy was not part of my name.
I gave as good as I got.
I had a chip on my shoulder.

My attitude was wrong from the start.
I got comfortable. God shook me up.

I was too comfortable with myself.
Did I know right from wrong?
I didn't want to be right.
How was that part of God's plan?
I got comfortable. God shook me up.

If you embed yourself in evil,
you become wicked.
You become comfortable
with doing you.
I don't want to be you.
I got comfortable. God shook me up.

I am more than an emotion.
I will not lose myself
to a sensation.
I am better than that.
Angry I am not.
I got comfortable. God shook me up.

If you get comfortable
in your feelings,
God will shake you up.
Learn to feel. Learn to care.

TAKEN

The feeling of sorrow.
What is this pain?
Most have experienced it.
Gone in the middle of night,
I cannot wake up.
Saddened by death, lifted by God.

I want to scream.
My tears won't stop.
How can this happen to me?
Saddened by death, lifted by God.

Does life just stop?
Did Jesus forget to breathe?
How can this be?
Dead by night.
My light went out.
Saddened by death, lifted by God.

Will my spirit linger on?
Stillness in my sleep, my body is cold.
I try to wake up.
Saddened by death, lifted by God.

Death was the thief
in the middle of the night.
I did not wake up.
My voice was silent.
Saddened by death, lifted by God.

Do not be sad;
those whom God takes he keeps.
Look at me looking down on you.
I already miss you.
Can I be your keeper in death?
Saddened by death, lifted by God.

Sad people will cry.
Hurt people must weep.
Will you cry?
I was saddened by my own death.
God has lifted me.
You may cry.
Saddened by death, lifted by God.

TEMPORARILY ON LOAN

Have you ever bought anything
on credit?
I took a loan.
It went into default.
Temporaily on loan,
my Father has called me home.

I thought I was the master
of my life.
I forgot that God was in control.
The hand of my brother King Jesus has
touched me,
a hand full of light
that shines so bright.
I took a loan.

It went into default.
Temporarily on loan,
my Father has called me home.

Who or what will I leave behind?
A life filled with joy and all my loved ones.
Please don't cry for me.
My loan and my time were up.
I took a loan.
It went into default.
Temporarily on loan,
my Father has called me home.

I smiled. I sang. I danced.
I lived my life to the fullest.
I did not cry.
Remember, I will see you again.
Look out, heaven, I'm coming home.
I took a loan.
It went into default.
Temporarily on loan,
my Father has called me home.

We all live on borrowed time.
Cry if you must.
Temporarily lost,
but we all find our way.

Living, loving, and losing are all parts
of the plan.
It was just another loan
that had to be paid.
Look up.
I am another star that twinkles in the sky.
Temporarily on loan,
my Father has called me home.

Recognizing

Someone asked me something
that she did not know.
"Will I recognize you
when I see you again?"

I laughed and grinned a little.
I said, "Of course, you will.
It will be me you see,
the young me."
Will I recognize you
when I see you again?

She asked me, "If I don't make it
to heaven, will I still live?"
I chuckled.
"Heaven is for a few.

Paradise is for many.
I will know you when I see you."
Will I recognize you
when I see you again?

Her next question was, "What if
you go to heaven, and
I remain behind?"
"I will visit you when I can.
I will see you again."
Will I recognize you
when I see you again?

My life and yours are important
to me.
I won't leave you behind.
Will I recognize you
when I see you again?

There are so many faces,
so many forms.
I will know you when I see you.

Recognizing,
searching with the eyes,
you see me.
Together we will be.

Part 9—Bonus Read

A THING OF BEAUTY

I cannot just choose one woman
to celebrate
because in my eyes
all women are worthy.
I am a woman. I am strong. I am worthy.

When God made woman,
he made something extraordinary.
We are the special ones.
We are a gift to all men.
I am a woman. I am strong. I am worthy.

We are the beautiful ones.
We are a sight to behold.
We carry God's grace.
We are gentle and kind.

I am a woman. I am strong. I am worthy.

We are creatures of wonder.
Our minds can never hold us back.
Remember, we think
with both sides of our brains.
We will go beyond
our limits for our loved ones.
I am a woman. I am strong. I am worthy.

We give birth to kings and queens.
We amaze the world.
Even men want to be us.
I am a woman. I am strong. I am worthy.

There are twelve months in a year.
If they give me one month
to celebrate all women.
I am thankful for all women
in the month of March.
I am a woman. I am strong. I am worthy.

Ladies, let's say this together:
"We are women. We are strong.
We are worthy. We will stand
and take our bow."

Celebrating women in the month of March

FREEDOM

I want to be free.
Slavery was a part of America.
It is a best-kept secret,
almost written out of
history books.
Does that make it right?
I want to be free. Let freedom rise.

What makes a slave?
The ownership of another.
I am a piece of paper
that carries a small value.
I want to be free. Let freedom rise.

Most of our grandparents
and great-grandparents were slaves.
No, I have never been a slave.
But do I have a slave mentality?
Yes to the master.
I want to be free. Let freedom rise.

When I was young,
I saw a black man
afraid of a white man.

I didn't understand why.
That was in the '80s.
Change came but not for him.
I want to be free. Let freedom rise.

Have the chains been broken?
We were emancipated on June 19, 1865.
When did the killings stop?
I want to be free. Let freedom rise.

Today I cannot be auctioned off as a slave.
I am free to live in America.
I will celebrate Juneteenth
in memory of those who could not see.

Happy June 19. We celebrate freedom.

Milton Keynes UK
Ingram Content Group UK Ltd.
UKHW020634210424
441371UK00006B/16

9 798822 942899